# FLYING HIGH

Search the sky for 10 differences
between these scenes.

# JOIN THE CIRCUS!

The circus is in town! Which of the shadow outlines is not an exact match for the performer?

# LOTS TO SPOT

# OUT AND ABOUT

by Genie Espinosa

WINDMILL
BOOKS

Published in 2020 by Windmill Books, an imprint of Rosen Publishing
29 East 21st Street, New York, NY 10010

Copyright © Arcturus Holdings Ltd, 2020

Illustrations: Genie Espinosa
Text: Paul Virr
Editors: Samantha Hilton and Joe Harris

Cataloging-in-Publication Data

Names: Espinosa, Genie.
Title: Out and about / Genie Espinosa.
Description: New York : Windmill Books, 2020.
| Series: Lots to spot
Identifiers: ISBN 9781538391648 (pbk.)
| ISBN 9781538391662 (library bound) | ISBN 9781538391655 (6 pack)
Subjects: LCSH: Picture puzzles–Juvenile literature.
Classification: LCC GV1507.P47 E875 2020 | DDC 793.73–dc23

Manufactured in the United States of America

CPSIA Compliance Information: Batch #BS19WM:
For Further Information contact Rosen Publishing,
New York, New York at 1-800-237-9932

# CONTENTS

| | | | | |
|---|---|---|---|---|
| Fun and Games | 4 | | Really Royal | 19 |
| Cooking Up a Storm | 6 | | Crazy Kitchen | 20 |
| Under Lock and Key | 7 | | Flying High | 21 |
| Candy Store | 8 | | Join the Circus! | 22 |
| Out of Tune | 10 | | Baboon on a Bike | 23 |
| Modern Art | 11 | | Happy New Year! | 24 |
| At the Mall | 12 | | Time for Tea | 26 |
| Flying the Flag | 14 | | Fancy That! | 27 |
| Keep on Running | 15 | | I Spy | 28 |
| Magic Show | 16 | | Night Night | 29 |
| Out of Step | 18 | | Answers | 30 |

## Step inside a world of awesome puzzles!

For some, you need to spot the differences between two
pictures. For others, you need to find the odd one out.
You'll find all the answers at the back of the book.
Turn the page to get started!

# FUN AND
# GAMES

# Step right up! Ride the roller coaster, then find 10 differences to win a prize!

# COOKING UP A STORM

Which of the chefs is armed with both a spoon and a saucepan?

# UNDER LOCK AND KEY

Each key opens a lock with matching decorations.
Which lock cannot be opened?

# CANDY STORE

Everything here looks yummy! Can you spot 10 differences between these sweet-toothed scenes?

# OUT OF TUNE

A member of the choir didn't read the dress code properly. Who has gotten it a little bit wrong?

# MODERN ART

Which of the forgeries has a mistake on it?

# AT THE MALL

# Get ready to shop and spot down at the mall. Can you find 10 differences?

# FLYING THE FLAG

Only one of these flags features an odd number of stars. Can you find it?

# KEEP ON RUNNING

Which of the athletes is running solo, rather than with other club members in matching tops?

# MAGIC
# SHOW

# Abracadabra! See if you can conjure up 10 differences between these magic show scenes.

# OUT OF STEP

Which dancer is a move behind the others?

# REALLY ROYAL

Begging your pardon, your Highness, but one of these pictures is not quite the same. Which one is it?

# CRAZY KITCHEN

Slice, dice, and spot 10 differences in the kitchen!